TO

FROM

DATE

GRANDMAS ARE SPECIAL PEOPLE

Artwork by

SUSAN WINGET

HARVEST HOUSE PUBLISHERS

EUGENE, OREGON

Grandmas are special people because they are...

Grandma, you're special because you know
that a great meal, conversation, or hug is
best served with an extra portion of love.

Don't judge each day by the harvest you reap,
but by the seeds you plant.

ROBERT LOUIS STEVENSON

GENEROUS

A grandma opens her arms wide to embrace the ones she loves. When her family visits, she stands on the porch with a wave and an eager smile. She can't wait for everyone to be together. She bends to scoop up the littlest family member and covers him with kisses. She winks to another child and points to the sunroom where a package adorned with yellow ribbon awaits.

Grandmas make everyone feel welcome. Moist, chewy oatmeal cookies and mouthwatering lemon cake appear as if by magic on the kitchen counter. And endless helpings of family favorites like cornbread and rosemary mashed potatoes flow at every meal.

Best of all, a grandma generously showers her family with love, prayer, and acceptance, and sends each person into the world with a refreshed, nurtured spirit.

Home is the resort of love, of joy, of peace, and plenty, where supporting and supported, polished friends and dearest relatives mingle into bliss.

JAMES THOMSON

The feeling of grandparents for their grandchildren can be expressed this way: "Our children are dear to us; but when we have grandchildren, they seem to be more dear than our children were." You might say that the grandmother falls all over herself to try to show her appreciation for her grandchild. It goes right back to those wishes that were made for them when they were little girls: the wish that they would live to become grandmothers someday.

HENRY OLD COYOTE

THE ONLY GIFT IS A PORTION OF THYSELF.

RALPH WALDO EMERSON

Every house where love abides and friendship is a guest, is surely home, and home, sweet home; for there the heart can rest.

HENRY VAN DYKE

HER PLEASURES ARE
IN THE HAPPINESS
OF HER FAMILY.

Jean Paul Rousseau

A grandma's name is little

Children are God's apostles, sent forth,
day by day, to preach of love, and hope and peace.

J.R. LOWELL

The heart hath its own memory, like the mind,
And in it are enshrined
The precious keepsakes, into which is wrought
The giver's loving thought.

HENRY WADSWORTH LONGFELLOW

*In this world, it is not what
we take up, but what we
give up, that makes us rich.*

HENRY WARD BEECHER

less in love than is the doting title of a mother.

WILLIAM SHAKESPEARE

9

Grandma, I love being silly with you.
You make me laugh, and you get my jokes.

What a bargain grandchildren are! I give them my loose change,
and they give me a million dollars' worth of pleasure.

GENE PERRET

JOYFUL

Laughter comes easily for grandmas. They are ready for the delight of jokes without good punch lines, stories without endings, and questions without answers. This is what life is all about! A grandma's attentive eyes and ears make her the best audience imaginable for each child, shy or bold.

Joy enriches the speech and actions of a grandma. Praises fall from her lips and blessings are lifted up to cover her family daily. She is quick to clap and cheer when milestones big or small are reached, and she is always ready to celebrate a child for any reason.

A grandma's positive outlook transforms her grandkids' experience. When the rain pours, she plans a picnic by the large-paned window and prepares a front row seat for the rainbow finale…another happy memory that promises a lifetime of joy.

Never fear spoiling children by making them too happy. Happiness is the atmosphere in which all good affections grow.

ANN BRAY

Who is not attracted by bright and pleasant children, to prattle, to creep, and to play with them?

EPICTETUS

If becoming a grandmother was only a matter of choice, I should advise every one of you straight away to become one. There is no fun for old people like it!

HANNAH WHITHALL SMITH

A HAPPY
FAMILY IS BUT
AN EARLIER
HEAVEN.

John Bowring

A GOOD LAUGH IS SUNSHINE IN A HOUSE.
WILLIAM MAKEPEACE THACKERAY

The haunts of happiness are varied, but I have more often found her among little children, home firesides, and country houses than anywhere else.

SYDNEY SMITH

14

Blessed be the hand that prepares a pleasure for a child, for there is no saying when and where it may bloom forth.

DOUGLAS WILLIAM JERROLD

The cheerful live longest in years,
and afterwards in our regards.
Cheerfulness is the offshoot of goodness.

CHRISTIAN NESTELL BOVEE

Childhood itself is scarcely
more lovely than a cheerful,
kindly, sunshiny old age.

LYDIA CHILD

15

Grandma, you're special because you explain things so that I understand them.

Let your grandchildren know through work and deeds, that the bond of affection which attaches the two of you to one another can never be broken.

ARTHUR KORNHABER

WISE

A grandma provides an open chair and an open invitation to talk. She listens patiently and then humbly shares wisdom from the year she felt lonely after her best friend moved, that summer when hard work earned her the sweetness of independence, and that season of trial when only faith could ease her heart.

Her antidote for a grandchild's concern could be a well-told anecdote. But it might emerge in the hush of prayer or the whir of a mixer as she selects a bread recipe that allows for plenty of talk time between cycles of kneading, rising, and baking.

A grandma mentors her grandchildren in conversations, in the way she puts people first, and in those casual notes she sends with a bit of spending money and a postscript with advice to listen to that still, small voice.

The interests
of childhood
and youth are
the interests
of mankind.

E.S. JANES

*Perfect love sometimes does not
come till the first grandchild.*

WELSH PROVERB

*The best school of discipline is
home—family life is God's
own method of training
the young; and homes are
very much what women
make them.*

SAMUEL SMILES

THE FAIREST
FLOWER IN
THE GARDEN
OF CREATION IS
A YOUNG MIND,
OFFERING AND
UNFOLDING
ITSELF TO THE
INFLUENCE
OF DIVINE
WISDOM, AS THE
HELIOTROPE
TURNS ITS SWEET
BLOSSOMS TO
THE SUN.

J.E. SMITH

An industrious and virtuous
education of children is
a better inheritance for
them than a great estate.

JOSEPH ADDISON

The true meaning of life is to plant trees, under whose shade you do not expect to sit.

NELSON HENDERSON

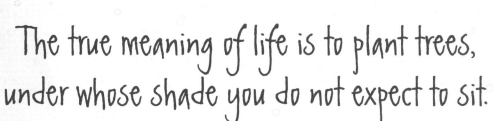

A good name
is rather to
be chosen than
great riches,
and loving favor
rather than
silver and gold.

SOLOMON

To make knowledge
valuable, you must
have the cheerfulness
of wisdom…Goodness
smiles to the last.

RALPH WALDO EMERSON

19

Grandma, you are my reminder
of how much God loves me.

*You can't live a perfect day without doing something
for someone who will never be able to repay you.*

JOHN WOODEN

LOVING

No one intuitively understands matters of the heart like a grandma. A grandma extends forgiveness, acceptance, and unconditional love to family, friends, neighbors, and to strangers she encounters from the bakery to the library. This hospitality and generosity permeates her life through her touch, her words, and her priorities. A person feels known and loved when she gives them the perfect gift or casts votes of confidence in them when they try something new.

A grandchild learns to emulate this active kindness. A grandson offers to carry the extra brown bag of groceries from the car. A granddaughter tilts her head with empathy and comforts her sad friend with a pat on the shoulder. Their wide eyes take in a grandmother's deliberate deeds of goodness. Their wide hearts take in a grandma's faith, love, and tenderness.

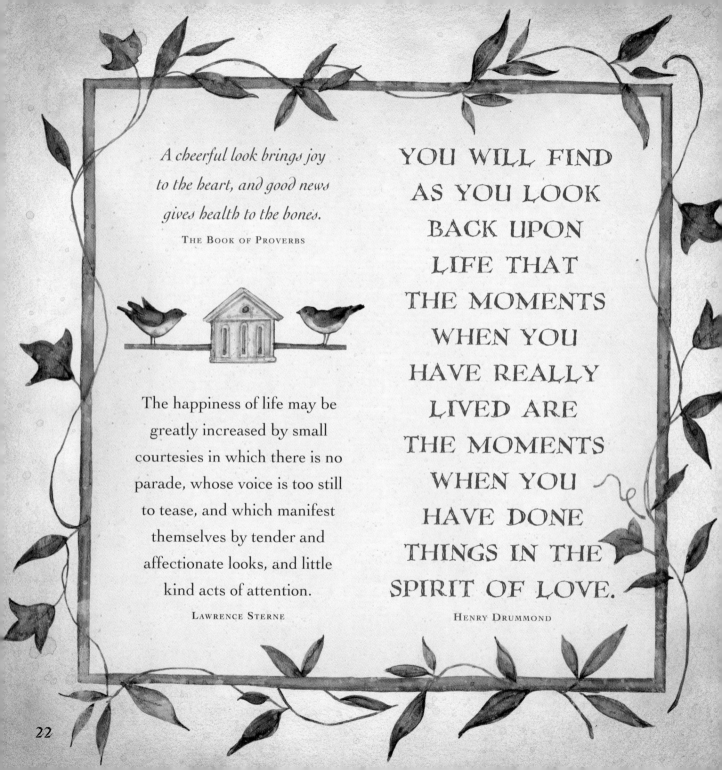

A cheerful look brings joy
to the heart, and good news
gives health to the bones.

THE BOOK OF PROVERBS

The happiness of life may be
greatly increased by small
courtesies in which there is no
parade, whose voice is too still
to tease, and which manifest
themselves by tender and
affectionate looks, and little
kind acts of attention.

LAWRENCE STERNE

YOU WILL FIND
AS YOU LOOK
BACK UPON
LIFE THAT
THE MOMENTS
WHEN YOU
HAVE REALLY
LIVED ARE
THE MOMENTS
WHEN YOU
HAVE DONE
THINGS IN THE
SPIRIT OF LOVE.

HENRY DRUMMOND

There never was any heart truly great and gracious,
that was not also tender and compassionate.

ROBERT SOUTH

How far you go
in life depends on
your being tender
with the young,
compassionate
with the aged,
sympathetic with
the striving and
tolerant of the
weak and strong.
Because someday
in your life you will
have been all of these.

GEORGE WASHINGTON CARVER

Every charitable act is a stepping stone toward heaven.

HENRY WARD BEECHER

I expect to pass through life but once. If therefore, there be any kindness I can show, or any good thing I can do to any fellow being, let me do it now, and not defer or neglect it, as I shall not pass this way again.

WILLIAM PENN

PHILANTHROPY, LIKE CHARITY, MUST BEGIN AT HOME; FROM THIS CENTER OUR SYMPATHIES SHOULD EXTEND IN AN EVER WIDENING CIRCLE.

CHARLES LAMB

Grandma, you're special because
your heart is as pretty as your smile.

Nobody can do for little children what grandparents do.
Grandparents sort of sprinkle stardust over the lives of little children.

ALEX HALEY

BEAUTIFUL

A grandma's beauty is refined by graciousness and gratitude. She has the ability to seek and find goodness wherever she goes. She's the first to notice the grandeur of the hills against the lavender sky. She lingers long enough to admire the intricate curl of a jasmine vine lacing the garden trellis. Her ability to recognize beauty extends as a gift of grace to her family as she pauses to witness and point out the potential and wonder of each child.

Her desire to savor moments and memories shapes a path to good living for her family. She invites them to follow her appreciation of the beauty found in creation, one another, and the harvest of life's gifts.

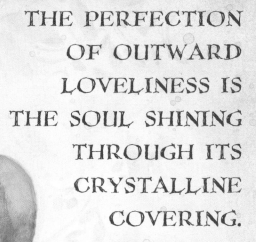

THE PERFECTION OF OUTWARD LOVELINESS IS THE SOUL SHINING THROUGH ITS CRYSTALLINE COVERING.

JANE PORTER

Every trait of beauty may be referred to some virtue, as to innocence, candor, generosity, modesty, or heroism.

SAINT PIERRE

Nature gives to every time and season some beauties of its own; and from morning to night, as from the cradle to the grave, is but a succession of changes so gentle and easy that we can scarcely mark their progress.

CHARLES DICKENS

28

Life is a flower of which love is the honey.

VICTOR HUGO

Beautiful is the activity which works for good,
and beautiful the stillness which waits
for good; blessed the self-sacrifice of one,
and blessed the self-forgetfulness
of the other.

ROBERT COLLYER

Goodness consists not in the outward things we do, but in the inward thing we are. To be good is the great thing.

E.H. CHAPIN

The best part of beauty is that which no picture can express.

FRANCIS BACON

30

A bit of fragrance always clings to the hand that gives roses.

CHINESE PROVERB

"Woman!" With that word,
Life's dearest hopes and memories come.
Truth, beauty, love, in her adored,
And earth's lost paradise restored,
In the green bower of home.

FITZGREEN HALLECK

A good and true woman is
said to resemble a Cremona
fiddle—age but increases its
worth and sweetens its tone.

OLIVER WENDELL HOLMES

WOMEN ARE THE POETRY OF THE WORLD IN THE SAME SENSE AS THE STARS ARE THE POETRY OF HEAVEN.

FRANCIS HARGRAVE

Grandma, you're special because you help me think through my questions, pray through the worries, and find the bright side of every circumstance.

When a child is born, so are grandmothers.

JUDITH LEVY

COMFORTING

Solace and refuge are found in the shelter of a grandma's presence. When a cut finger, imperfect craft project, or a broken heart is brought to a grandma's attention, her simple "um-hmm" extends the deepest understanding. Like a cool hand to a feverish forehead, a grandma's touch is a balm to soothe any hurt.

When a family is blessed with a newborn, a grandma is blessed with an ample supply of love and kisses for that very child. When their tears start to trickle, her prayers and sweet songs begin to flow.

A grandma knows that it's silly to measure a child's pain or the weight of their mistake because every trouble calls for one and only one remedy dosage: unlimited, unconditional love.

Our sweetest experiences of affection are meant to point us to that realm which is the real and endless home of the heart.

HENRY WARD BEECHER

Charity sees the need, not the cause.

GERMAN PROVERB

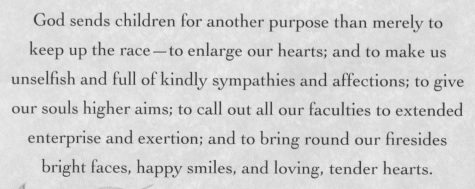

God sends children for another purpose than merely to keep up the race—to enlarge our hearts; and to make us unselfish and full of kindly sympathies and affections; to give our souls higher aims; to call out all our faculties to extended enterprise and exertion; and to bring round our firesides bright faces, happy smiles, and loving, tender hearts.

MARY HOWITT

One's age should be tranquil, as childhood should be playful. Hard work at either extremity of life seems out of place. At midday the sun may burn, and men labor under it; but the morning and evening should be alike calm and cheerful.

THOMAS ARNOLD

I LOVE THESE
LITTLE PEOPLE;
AND IT IS NOT
A SLIGHT THING,
WHEN THEY
WHO ARE SO
FRESH FROM
GOD LOVE US.

CHARLES DICKENS

Children are the hands by which we take hold of heaven.

HENRY WARD BEECHER

Life is made up,
not of great
sacrifices or duties,
but of little things
in which smiles,
and kindnesses,
and small obligations,
given habitually,
are what win and
preserve the heart
and secure comfort.

SIR H. DAVY

WE HAVE TWO
EARS AND ONE
MOUTH SO THAT
WE CAN LISTEN
TWICE AS MUCH
AS WE SPEAK.

EPICTETUS

Be ever gentle with the children God has given you.

ELIHU BURRITT

Mid pleasures and palaces though we may roam,

Be it ever so humble, there's no place like home;

A charm from the sky seems to hallow us there,

Which, seek through the world, is ne'er met with elsewhere.

Home, home, sweet, sweet home!

There's no place like home, oh,

There's no place like home.

JOHN HOWARD PAYNE

Grandma, I know you're my grandma
because you always know just
what I need...even when I'm not sure!

The smallest children are nearest to God,
as the smallest planets are nearest the sun.

JEAN PAUL RICHTER

FAITHFUL

A grandma's heart beats for her family and for those dear to her. Grandma has a gift for sensing what her grandkids need anytime and anywhere. Sometimes it's a hug, a role model, a letter of encouragement. Sometimes it's a round of sharing and laughing while folding chocolate batter into cupcake tins — or eating peppermint frosting right out of a can when the parents aren't looking!

The faithfulness of a grandmother's heart is perhaps experienced most fully through the prayers she continuously lifts up for her family. When her prayers are spoken over her grandchildren, each child feels a renewed sense of God's care. A grandma's prayers are special because they always remind her family that God's presence and peace are as sure as her warm embrace.

Moral courage is a virtue of higher cast and nobler origin than physical. It springs from a consciousness of virtue, and renders a man, in the pursuit or defense of right, superior to the fear of reproach, opposition, or contempt.

S.G. GOODRICH

A HOUSE WITHOUT A
ROOF WOULD SCARCELY
BE A MORE DIFFERENT
HOME THAN A FAMILY
UNSHELTERED BY GOD'S
FRIENDSHIP, AND THE SENSE
OF BEING ALWAYS RESTED
IN HIS PROVIDENTIAL CARE
AND GUIDANCE.

HORACE BUSHNELL

If God be there, a cottage
will hold as much happiness
as might stock a palace.

J. HAMILTON

Blessed be God, I not only begin praying when I kneel
down, but I do not leave off praying when I rise up.

T. ADAM

There cannot be a more glorious object in
creation than a human being replete with
benevolence, meditating in what manner
he may render himself most acceptable to
the Creator by doing good to his creatures.

HENRY FIELDING

He prayeth best who loveth best.

SAMUEL TAYLOR COLERIDGE

For the Lord is good.
His unfailing love continues forever,
And his faithfulness continues to each generation.

THE BOOK OF PSALMS

THE EVENING OF A WELL-SPENT LIFE BRINGS ITS LAMPS WITH IT.

JOSEPH JOUBERT

If God has taught us all truth in teaching us to love, then he has given us an interpretation of our whole duty to our households.

HENRY WARD BEECHER

The sweetest type of heaven is home.

J.G. HOLLAND

Grandma, is there anything you can't do?
You're amazing.

ONE OF A KIND

"Nobody can compare to my grandma."

"Nana is the best friend anyone ever had."

"My grandma can juggle four apples while whistling the 'Star Spangled Banner.'"

"The only meal worth eating is my grandmother's meatloaf."

When it comes to grandmas, there is no doubt that each one is remarkable and unique. Who else would create a casserole recipe using all her grandchild's favorite ingredients—*even* the extra spicy taco sauce? Who, but Nana, will go through every box in the attic until she finds her favorite childhood chapter book to present to her grandson graduating third grade? Who, but Grandma, will still send a note and some spending money "just because" when her granddaughter is promoted to CEO?

If anyone were to ask "What's so great about a grandma?" a flurry of one-of-a-kind responses would be heard around the world. And that's because the greatest thing about a grandma is that she loves her grandchild in her own special way.

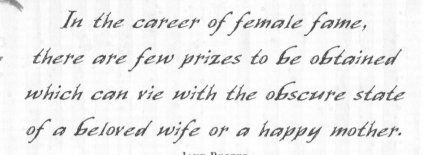

In the career of female fame,
there are few prizes to be obtained
which can vie with the obscure state
of a beloved wife or a happy mother.

JANE PORTER

A life spent worthily
should be measured
by deeds, not years.

R.B. SHERIDAN

We need not power or
splendor; wide hall or
lordly dome; the good,
the true, the tender, these form
the wealth of home.

SARA HALE

A GOOD HEART,
BENEVOLENT
FEELINGS, AND A
BALANCED MIND LIE
AT THE FOUNDATION
OF CHARACTER.
OTHER THINGS
MAY BE DEEMED
FORTUITOUS; THEY
MAY COME AND GO;
BUT CHARACTER
IS THAT WHICH
LIVES AND ABIDES
AND IS ADMIRED
LONG AFTER ITS
POSSESSOR HAS LEFT
THE EARTH.

JOHN TODD

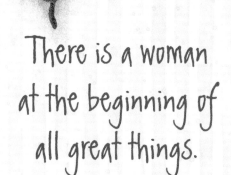

There is a woman
at the beginning of
all great things.

ALPHONSE DE LAMARTINE

47

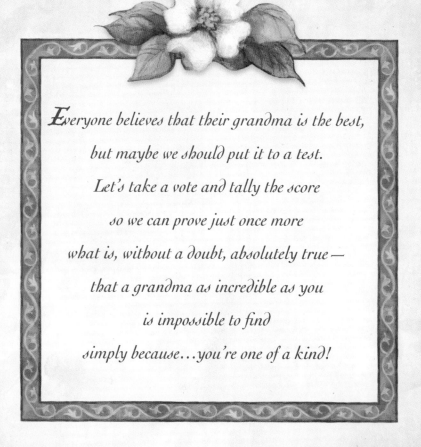

Everyone believes that their grandma is the best,

but maybe we should put it to a test.

Let's take a vote and tally the score

so we can prove just once more

what is, without a doubt, absolutely true—

that a grandma as incredible as you

is impossible to find

simply because…you're one of a kind!